Edward Lear

There was an Old Man of Moldavia,
Who had the most curious behavior;
For while he was able, he slept on a table,
That funny Old Man of Moldavia.

old
Lică
Sainciuc

Edward Lear

Nonsense Alphabet

papà — **Lică Sainciuc**

Chisinau
1978 — 2021

Anteater

C was Papa's grey Cat,
  Who caught a squeaky Mouse;
She pulled him by his twirly tail
  All about the house.

D

D was Papa's white Duck,

    Who had a curly tail;

One day it ate a great fat frog,

    Besides a leetle snail.

E was a little Egg
   Upon the breakfast table;
Papa came in and ate it up,
   As fast as he was able.

F was a little fish.
Cook in the river took it,
Papa said,"Cook! Cook! bring a dish!
And, Cook! be quick and cook it!"

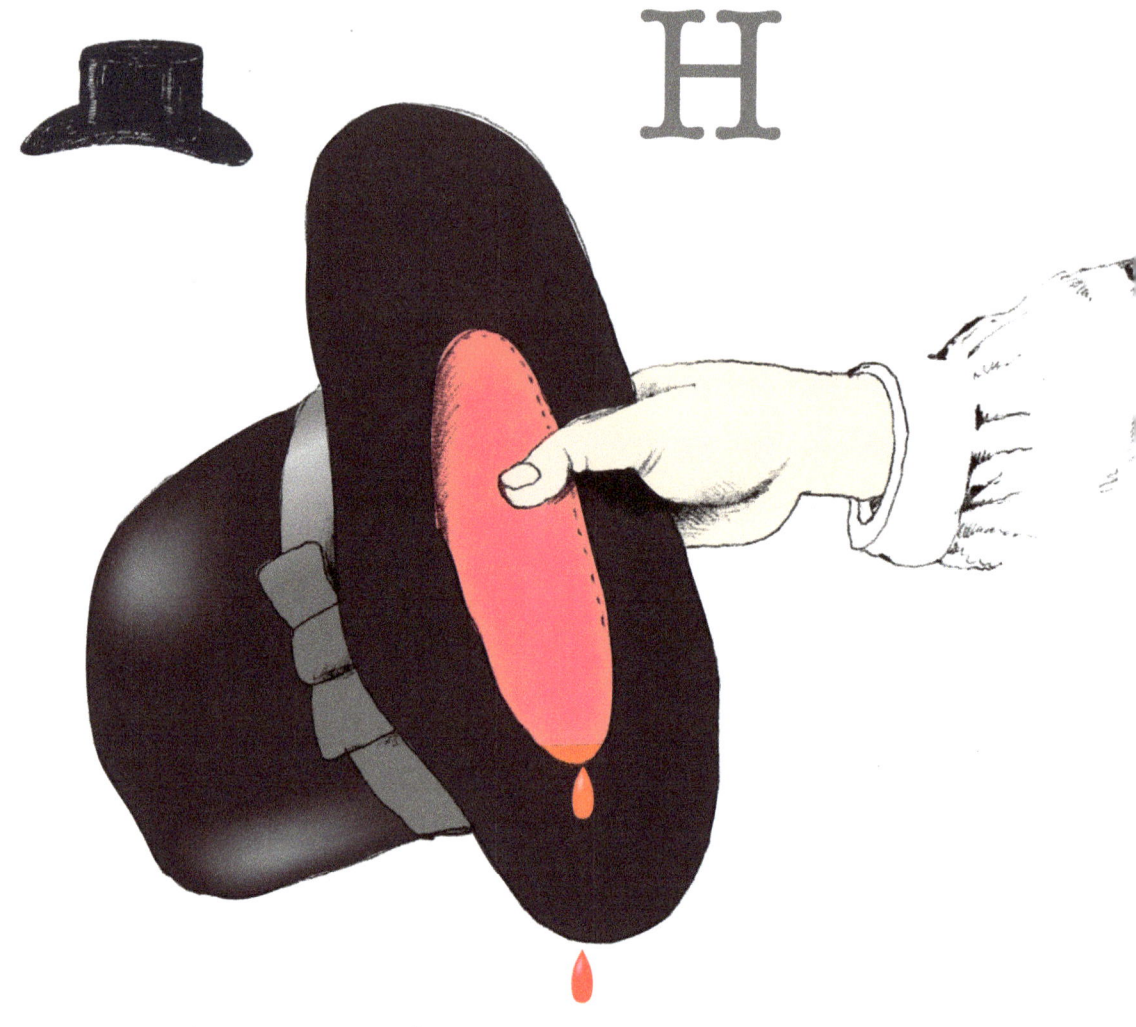

H was Papa's new Hat;

He wore it on his head;

Outside it was completely black,

But inside it was red.

I was an Inkstand new,
   Papa he likes to use it;
He keeps it in his pocket now,
   For fear that he should lose it.

J was some Apple Jam,
   Of which Papa ate part,
   But all the rest he took away,
   And stuffed into a tart.

K was a great new Kite;
Papa he saw it fly
Above a thousand chimney pots,
And all about the sky.

L was a fine new Lamp;
    But when the wick was lit,
Papa he said,"This light ain't good!
    I cannot read a bit!"

M

M was a dish of Mince;
    It looked so good to eat!
Papa he quickly ate it up,
    And said,"This is a treat!"

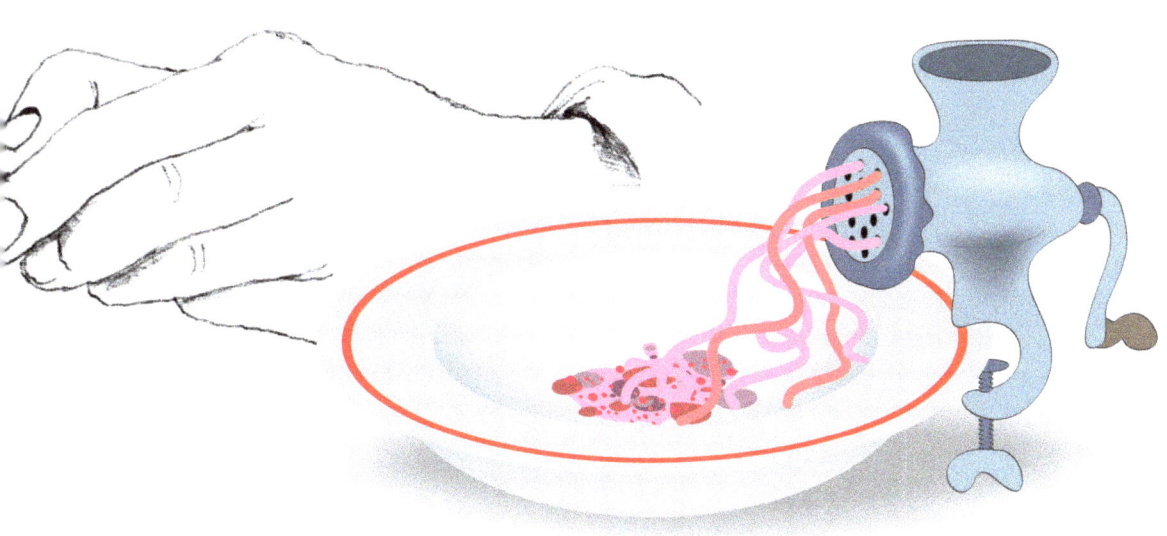

 P

P was a little Pig,
    Went out to take a walk;
Papa he said,"If Piggy dead,
    He'd all turn into Pork!"

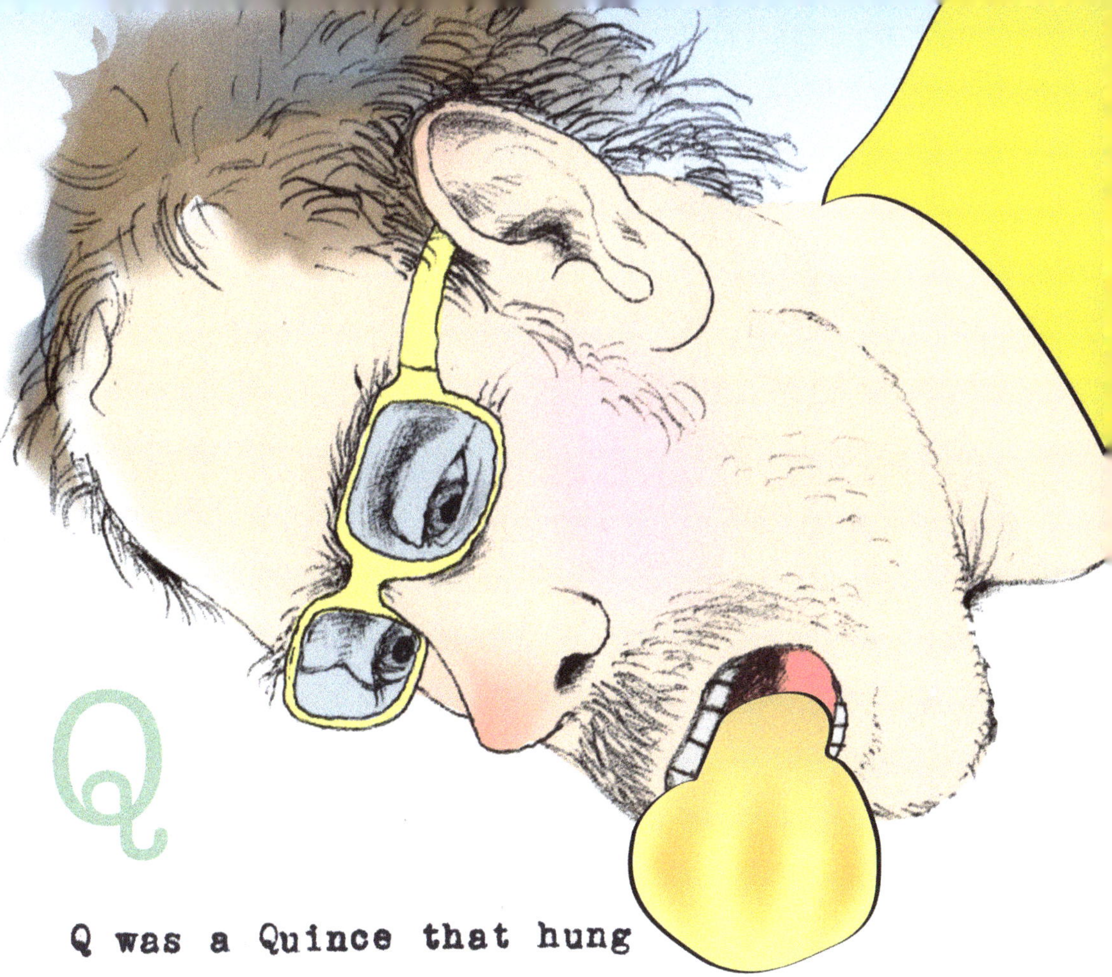

Q

Q was a Quince that hung

    Upon a garden tree;

Papa he brought it with him home,

    And ate it with his tea.

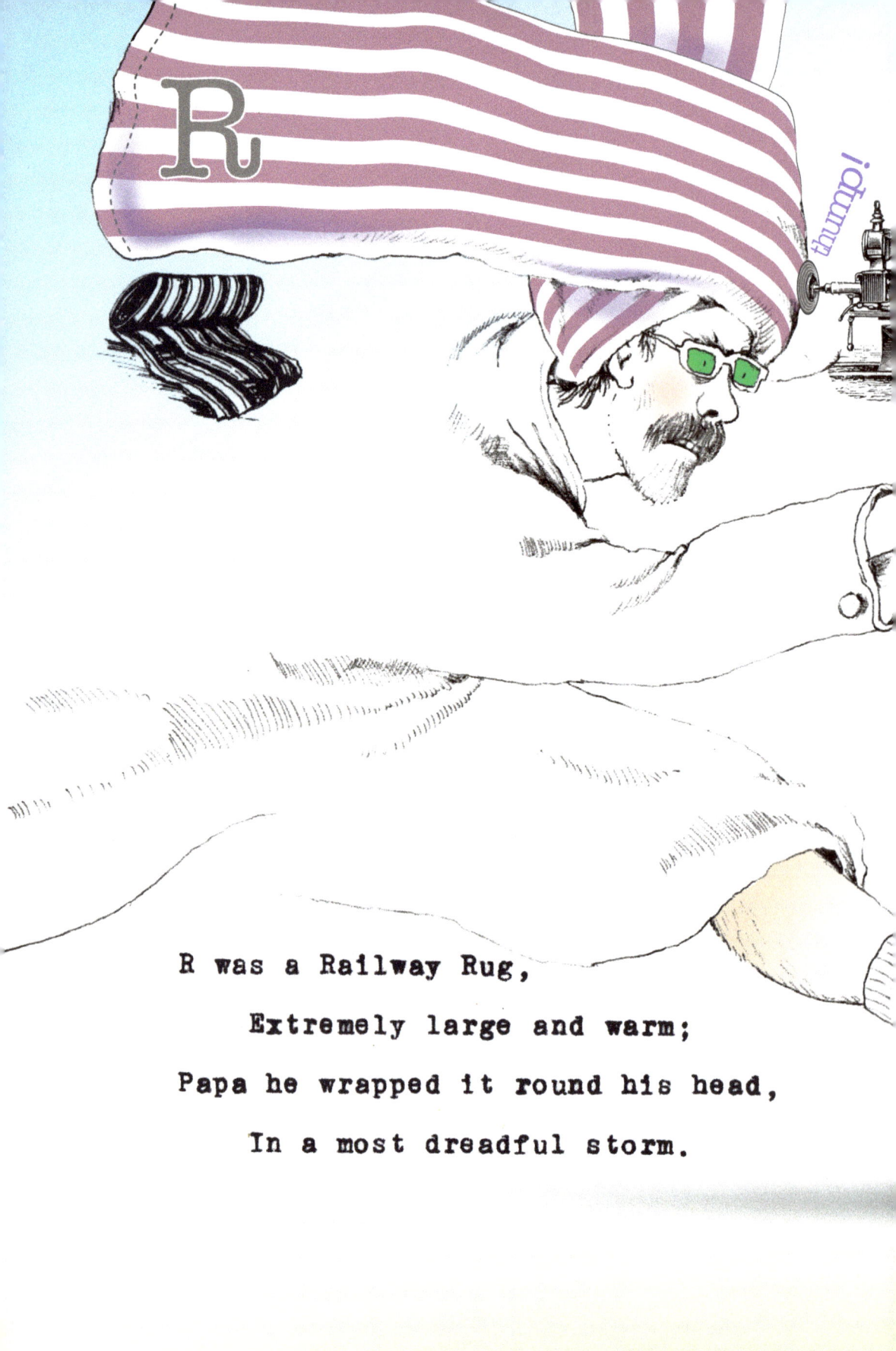

R was a Railway Rug,

    Extremely large and warm;

Papa he wrapped it round his head,

    In a most dreadful storm.

S

S was Papa's new Stick,

    Papa's new thumping Stick,

To thump extremely wicked boys,

    Because it was so thick.

T was a Tumbler full
   Of Punch all hot and good,
Papa he drank it up, when in
   The middle of a wood.

U

U was a silver Urn,
    Full of hot scalding water;
Papa he said,"If that Urn were mine,
    I'd give it to my daughter!"

V was a Villain; once
    He stole a piece of beef.
Papa he said,"O! dreadful man!
    That Villain is a Thief!"

W

W was a Watch of Gold:

    It told the time of day,

So Papa knew when to come,

    And when to go away.

X was King Xerxes, whom
    Papa much wished to know;
But this he could not do, because
    Xerxes died long ago.

Y was a Youth, who kicked
    And screamed and cried like mad;
Papa he said, "Your conduct is
    Abominably bad!"

Z

Z was a Zebra striped
    And streaked with lines of black;
Papa said once, he thought he'd like
    A ride apon his back.

The End

Papa he said, " My little Boy!
My little Boy so dear!
This Alphabet was made for you,
By Mr Edward Lear.
And should you ever meet with him,
This is his picture here."
Papa he said, — " This really does
Resemble,

      Edward Lear."

some drawings by Edward Lear

London 1849

Edward Lear
Nonsense Alphabet

Undertable Library

other drawings by © **Lică Sainciuc**

www.ingramcontent.com/pod-product-compliance
Lightning Source LLC
Chambersburg PA
CBHW061127170426
43209CB00014B/1696